A beginner's guide to

LangGraph

and

Daniel Nastase

1. Introduction

1.1. Getting Book Updates and Code Examples

To get the most recent versions of the book, join the mailing list by emailing daniel @js-craft.io. I'm committed to keeping the book up-to-date with the latest developments in LangGraph, LangChain and other libraries. I frequently update the code and content, so subscribing will ensure you're always in the loop.

For access to the complete source code for all the projects, or to receive the PDF version of the book, just drop me a message at daniel@js-craft.io.

1.2. Requirements and How to Use This Book

LangChain and LangGraph offer implementations in both JavaScript and Python. The actual version is not very important as all the described concepts are the same in both languages.

You'll find that you learn best by coding along with the examples provided in the book. My suggestion is to initially go through each chapter, absorbing the content to grasp the concepts. Then, during a second pass, code along as you progress.

Throughout this book, our focus will be on the JavaScript version.

We'll utilize a combination of LangGraph, LangChain, and Node. While a basic understanding of JavaScript is expected, you need not be an expert.

For setting up Node, the simplest approach is to utilize a version manager like NVM (Node Version Manager). This allows you to easily install, update, and switch between different Node versions without any hassle.

The examples will progress in a step-by-step iterative manner. Each modification will be denoted and explained.

Please note that both LangGraph and LangChain are currently undergoing development and are chaining rapidly. While I'll strive to update the book frequently, there might be brief periods where method names or import statements are not aligned with the latest version.

For support, feel free to reach out via email at daniel@js-craft.io.

1.3. Overview

AI agents are here to stay, and LangGraph makes it easy to build them and harness their capabilities!

Today's Large Language Models (LLMs) are impressive, but let's be real. These LLMs are still primarily just sophisticated text processors.

So, how can we evolve these text processors into autonomous problem solvers that can understand and interact with the world around them?

Enter AI agents. Simply put, AI agents are LLMs that operate in a loop to accomplish specific goals.

You can assign them tasks such as:

- a calendar manager to schedule and manage appointments, send reminders, and suggest optimal meeting times
- a personal AI agent assistant to organize trips, and book hotels or plane tickets for a destination on a given budget.

These are much closer to the capabilities we expect from real AI.

AI agents are LLMs on steroids. The anatomy of an agent consists of the following parts:

- the LLM used for decision making
- memory support for context
- tools to interact with the environment
- do while loop
- and planning

The LangGraph framework is an excellent tool for implementing and orchestrating all of these components.

AI agents can solve very complex situations thus clear communication is essential to achieve the desired results.

This is where LangGraph excels. Communicating with LLMs via code leads to far more reliable results than using only natural language (prompt engineering).

In this book, we'll take you on a fun, hands-on journey where each chapter will focus on essential concepts like tool management or human in the loop validation, while also coding practical implementations of these elements using LangGraph.

You can see this book as your launchpad. You'll build your first AI agent within minutes, and slowly become competent and knowledgeable in this technology, with each chapter featuring a full practical example.

Let's start learning!

2. AI Agents

2.1. So, What Are AI Agents?

We will start with the million dollar question: "What is an AI agent?".

Everyone seems to have a slightly different definition of what an AI agent is.

I like the definition given by Harrison Chase, the co-founder of LangChain:

> An AI agent is a system that uses an LLM to decide the control flow of an application.

I feel this is one of the most clean definitions. You can read the full article here: https://blog.langchain.dev/what-is-an-agent/

But how can we use an LLM to decide the control flow of an application?

Well, very often Large Language Models are referenced as "glorified autocompletes". You will give to an LLM an array of words such as "Mike is quick he moves ...", and the LLM will add the word "fast".

For decision-making, we can use the same autocomplete mechanism.

Let's say you pass to the LLM the input "I have a chainsaw and a screwdriver. To cut down a tree I will use the ... ". The LLM will respond with "chainsaw".

But, in this case, the autocomplete done by the LLM also functioned as a decision. It decided we could use the chainsaw tool to achieve the objective.

By the way, the "Mike is quick he moves ..." is an example given by Ishan Anand, in this fantastic talk Decoding the Decoder LLM https://youtu.be/NamKkerrlnQ. I highly recommend you watch that talk if you want to get a deeper understanding of the technical inner workings of LLMs.

In a very simple way we can see AI agents as a sum of the following parts:

An LLM with looping, termination, and tools is usually considered an AI agent. A system that loops on the same prompt, or some set of prompts, plus it has the ability to continue execution and then decide when it wants to stop that is an AI agent.

If you want to read more, Shawn Swyx Wang, the host of the Latent Space podcast and the one who coined the AI Engineer role, wrote a really good article on AI agents https://www.latent.space/p/agents

Picture the following scenario. You open up your computer and type in the following prompt into your favorite LLM:

```
This weekend I want to do a hiking trip in the south of France!
Please arrange all the details for me.
```

A typical LLM might respond:

```
I apologize, but as a language model, I'm unable to actually make
travel arrangements or bookings for you.
```

And for good reasons. The LLM would need various pieces of information and capabilities to achieve this objective. For example:

- your current location
- a web browser to check if the weather is suitable for a hiking trip
- a way to book your plane tickets and hotel

- a way to call for a taxi to take you to the airport and hotel

The actions the LLM can take to reach its goals are represented by tools. Tools are typically code functions that allow the LLM to call APIs, browse the web, read or write files on your local machine, and more.

The flow of this personal assistant AI agent is illustrated in the diagram below:

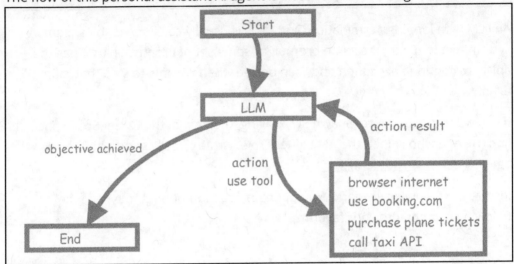

But where does LangGraph fit into this picture? Well, we will explore that in the next chapter.

2.2. Meet Your New Best Friend: LangGraph

LangGraph is a framework developed by the same company that created LangChain. Its purpose is to simplify how we build, interact with, and manage AI agents.

I will refer again to the words of Harrison Chase (co-founder of LangChain) to describe the role of LangGraph: "I think at the end of the day, what it all comes down to is communication. If there's some agent that's doing something, we need to communicate to it how we want it to behave."

If you're interested, you can watch the full interview with him here: https://youtu.be/S9cz94jgZ4c.

Sometimes, a simple prompt is enough to guide an AI, but code is a more powerful communicator. Code can be more precise, cost-effective, and provide better structure.

AI using code is way more powerful than AI just using language, aka prompt engineering.

This is exactly where LangGraph fits into the AI agent landscape.

LangGraph aims to provide a straightforward way to define and orchestrate the behavior of AI agents. It offers easy-to-use mechanisms for tasks such as:

- describing the flow of how an AI agent should act
- building the toolbox an AI agent needed to achieve its objectives
- helping the AI agent manage different conversation threads
- human in the loop confirmations
- first-class support for streaming
- and much more

One of the best features of LangGraph is that it avoids hidden prompts, making everything cleaner and easier to manage.

And just like LangChain, LangGraph is available in two versions: JavaScript and Python.

Let's start by exploring the fundamental concepts that define how LangGraph works.

3. LangGraph Fundamentals

3.1. Introduction

In this chapter, we will explore the foundational building blocks of graph structures used to define AI agents and their behavior.

While the first part of this example may seem simple, a good understanding of the topics discussed will help as we progress.

Keep an eye on the next chapter, where we will add LLMs and AI agents into the mix to build more practical examples.

In this chapter we will go through the following:

- installing LangGraph
- using Nodes, Edges, and Graphs
- defining Conditional Edges and Cycles

3.2. Installing LangGraph

Before we can create our first graphs, we need to ensure LangGraph and LangChain are installed.

For now, you won't need an OpenAI API key, so you can skip that part.

Before we start, ensure that Node.js and NPM are installed on your machine.

We'll begin by creating a new folder to host our files:

```
mkdir langgraph-first
cd langgraph-first
```

The first step is to initialize the Node app. Run the following commands in the `langgraph-first` folder:

```
npm init -y
npm install @langchain/langgraph @langchain/core
```

Next, create a `index.js` file. This file will store the main LangGraph code.

Once the initialization is complete the libraries will be added to the `package.json` file. At this point, your `langgraph-first` folder should contain the following files:

```
langchain-node
    ├── node_modules
    ├── index.js
    ├── package-lock.json
    └── package.json
```

Before running this code, we need to configure Node.js to use import statements. To do this, open `package.json` and add the following line to the root object:

```
"type": "module",
```

With everything set up, we can run our example using:

```
node index.js
```

3.3. Nodes, Edges, and Graphs in LangGraph

Graphs are an ideal data structure to describe a logical schema that encapsulates the behavior of an AI agent.

Let's define a simple structure like this:

```
START --> nodeA --> nodeB --> END
```

In a real life scenario nodeA and nodeB will represent actions taken by the Agent.

Each node will be a function that gets executed when we reach that node. The nodes will be linked in a coherent structure using edges.

Here's how it looks in code:

```
import { END, START, MessageGraph } from "@langchain/langgraph"
import * as fs from "fs"

const funcA = input => {
  input[0].content += "Agent takes action A; ";
  return input
}
const funcB = input => {
  input[0].content += "Agent takes action B; ";
  return input
}

// build the graph
const graph = new MessageGraph()
    // nodes
    .addNode("nodeA", funcA)
    .addNode("nodeB", funcB)
    // edges
```

```
    .addEdge(START, "nodeA")
    .addEdge("nodeA", "nodeB")
    .addEdge("nodeB", END)

const runnable = graph.compile()
const result = await runnable.invoke('Input; ')
console.log(result)
```

Both START and END are simple string constants indicating the entry and exit points of the graph.

The flow is straightforward: we move from nodeA to nodeB, with each node adding something to the initial input.

The result of running the code:

```
[
  HumanMessage {
    "id": "675cb46c-2637-4ea5-ad35-1cde12615e49",
    "content": "Input; Agent takes action A; Agent takes action
B;",
    "additional_kwargs": {},
    "response_metadata": {}
  }
]
```

Since LangGraph uses LangChain's runnables, we can easily chain multiple calls, much like in the old days of jQuery:

```
const graph = new MessageGraph()
    .addNode(...)
    .addNode(...)
    .addEdge(...)
    .addEdge(...)
```

In a future subchapter, we will see how easy it is to render the graph structure as an image.

3.4. Conditional Edges in LangGraph

In addition to simple direct edges, LangGraph allows for conditional edges.

Using conditional edges, the flow of the graph can be routed through different parts of the graph based on a given condition.

Here's some code that builds a graph with two conditional edges:

```javascript
import { END, START, MessageGraph } from '@langchain/langgraph'

const funBuy = input => {
    input[0].content += " ==> Agent will buy stocks"
    return input
}

const funSell = input => {
    input[0].content += " ==> Agent will sell stocks"
    return input
}

const funDecision = input => {
    const last = input[0].content
    const isMarketDown = last.includes("SP500") &&
last.includes("down")
    return isMarketDown ?
        "actionBuyStocks":
        "actionSellSocks"
}

const graph = new MessageGraph()

// setup nodes
graph.addNode("decision", funDecision)
```

```
    .addNode("actionBuyStocks", funBuy)
    .addNode("actionSellSocks", funSell)

// setup edges
graph.addEdge(START, "decision")
    .addConditionalEdges(
        "decision",
        funDecision,
        ["actionBuyStocks", "actionSellSocks"]
    )
    .addEdge("actionBuyStocks", END)
    .addEdge("actionSellSocks", END)

const runnable = graph.compile()
const result = await runnable.invoke("Latest news SP500 is down to
5000")
console.log(result)
```

Based on the result of the decision, if the initial input indicates that the stock market is down, the AI agent will buy stocks. Otherwise, it will execute sell stock , adding the respective markers to the output.

This is the final output:

```
HumanMessage {
    "id": "c6e0e2fe-bb8b-494b-a019-bd54ad7cbbf4",
    "content": "Latest news SP500 is up to 5000 ==> Agent will
sell stocks",
    "additional_kwargs": {},
    "response_metadata": {}
}
```

3.5. Cycles

So far, most of what we've done in this tutorial could also be achieved with LCEL - LangChain Expression Language.

However, creating cycles (or loops) is not possible within LCEL.

We can think of AI agents as LLMs running in a `do-while` loop until they achieve a specific objective. We provide an AI agent with an objective and a set of tools, and it loops through different strategies to accomplish the objective.

Therefore, cycles are a crucial component in describing AI agent behavior with LangGraph.

Let's simulate an AI agent with the following:

- An objective: roll a 6 with a dice
- A dice tool that can roll any number between 1 and 6

The idea is to keep rolling the dice until the agent reaches its objective.

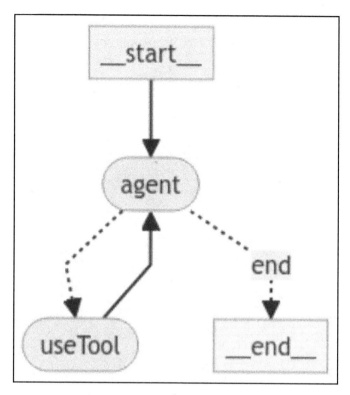

Here it is how it will look like in JavaScript:

```javascript
import { END, START, MessageGraph } from '@langchain/langgraph'
import { HumanMessage } from '@langchain/core/messages'

const funAgent = input => input
const funUseDiceTool = input => {
    const dice = 1 + Math.floor(Math.random() * 6)
    const content = (dice !== 6) ?
        'Dice rolled: ' + dice :
        'objective_achieved'
    input.push(new HumanMessage(content))
    return input
}
```

```javascript
const shouldContinue = input => {
    return input.pop().content.includes('objective_achieved') ?
        'end' :
        'useDiceTool'
}

const graph = new MessageGraph()

// setup nodes
graph.addNode('agent', funAgent)
    .addNode('useDiceTool', funUseDiceTool)

// setup edges
graph.addEdge(START, 'agent')
    .addEdge('useDiceTool', 'agent')
    .addConditionalEdges(
        'agent',
        shouldContinue,
        {'useDiceTool': 'useDiceTool', 'end': END}
    )

const runnable = graph.compile()
const result = await runnable.invoke('Start game')
console.log(result)
```

As you can see there isn't a new special type of edge we add. We are building a cycle by using a simple conditional edge.

Here's an example of the output:

```
[
  HumanMessage {
    "id": "3ad9e1fa-9c93-47aa-aa7d-045286179765",
    "content": "Start game",
```

```
        "additional_kwargs": {},
        "response_metadata": {}
    },
    HumanMessage {
        "id": "c08ea29e-39b4-4cd1-9216-10357cd569b7",
        "content": "Dice rolled: 3",
        "additional_kwargs": {},
        "response_metadata": {}
    },
    HumanMessage {
        "id": "053a44d1-1155-45ba-abfb-67b952086277",
        "content": "objective_achieved",
        "additional_kwargs": {},
        "response_metadata": {}
    }
]
```

3.6. Visualize the Graph

For more complex graph structures, LangGraph provides some very useful visualization tools.

Take the example below:

```
import { END, START, MessageGraph } from "@langchain/langgraph"
import * as fs from "fs"

// define the nodes
const funcA = input => { input[0].content += "A"; return input }
const funcB = input => { input[0].content += "B"; return input }
const funcC = input => { input[0].content += "C"; return input }
const funcD = input => { input[0].content += "D"; return input }
const funcE = input => { input[0].content += "E"; return input }

const graph = new MessageGraph()

// build nodes
graph.addNode("nodeA", funcA)
graph.addNode("nodeB", funcB)
graph.addNode("nodeC", funcC)
graph.addNode("nodeD", funcD)
graph.addNode("funcE", funcE)

// add node connections using edges
graph.addEdge(START, "nodeA")
graph.addEdge("nodeA", "nodeB")
graph.addEdge("nodeA", "nodeC")
graph.addEdge("nodeA", "nodeD")
graph.addEdge("nodeB", "funcE")
graph.addEdge("nodeC", "funcE")
graph.addEdge("nodeD", "funcE")
```

```
graph.addEdge("funcE", END)

// printing the graph as a PNG image
const FILE_NAME = "graph-struct.png"
const runnable = graph.compile()
const image = await runnable.getGraph().drawMermaidPng();
const arrayBuffer = await image.arrayBuffer();
await fs.writeFileSync(FILE_NAME, new Uint8Array(arrayBuffer))
console.log("Graph structure exported to: " + FILE_NAME)
```

This graph is a bit more complex than the previous examples. We have 5 nodes, and in the real world, the structures used to define agent behavior can go much deeper.

Luckily, using the drawing methods from LangGraph, we get clear visual representations of these graph structures.

Running the above code will generate this PNG diagram, where we can easily track the flow and structure of the graph:

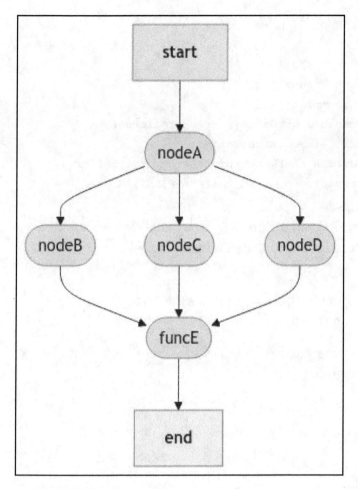

This works with any type of graph, including the state graphs we will discuss in a future chapter.

And there you have it! These are the fundamental building blocks for defining graphs with LangGraph.

In the next chapter, we will see how to add an LLM to the graph to build a real AI agent.

4. Building Your First AI Agent

4.1. Introduction

Let's see how we can use LangGraph to build a personal assistant AI agent powered by OpenAI's ChatGPT.

The AI agent will help us to make a phone call to someone who lives in another timezone. For example, if we pass it an input like the one below:

```
"What is the time now in Singapore? I would like to call a friend
who lives there."
```

We will receive an answer like this:

```
"AI: The current time in Singapore is 2:30 AM. It is too early for
a call!"
```

In this chapter, we will cover the following topics:

- defining a graph for an AI agent using LangGraph.js
- setting up tools for the AI agent
- interpreting the various results using the AI agent
- dealing with failing API calls

4.2. Setting Up the Environment

To begin, you'll need to install the necessary libraries. Here's a quick setup:

```
npm install @langchain/core @langchain/langgraph @langchain/openai
zod dotenv
```

To use OpenAI's ChatGPT model, you will need an API key. The API is subscription-based and the key can be generated from the following URL:

```
https://platform.openai.com/api-keys
```

You can top up your account with the minimum value. For example, writing all the examples in this book cost me under 0.5 USD.

Once you've generated your API key, return to the project and paste it into the `.env` file:

```
// .env file
OPENAI_API_KEY=sk-1234567890
```

Once this is ready you load your environment variables using `dotenv`:

```
import * as dotenv from "dotenv"
dotenv.config({ path: '../.env' })
```

The `dotenv.config()` line will make sure the `OPENAI_API_KEY` value will be later passed to the `ChatOpenAI` instance object.

4.3. Initialize ChatOpenAI and Define the Tools

We'll use a `ChatOpenAI` object from LangChain to drive the AI's conversation. By setting the temperature to 0, the model produces more predictable and deterministic responses:

```
const llm = new ChatOpenAI({ model: "gpt-4o", temperature: 0 })
```

We will create a custom tool to check the local time in a specific city.

Tools are code pieces that can be used by the LLM to interact with its surroundings. Using tools the LLM can get real time data from APIs, get access to files, run other programs and so on.

In this case, the scope of the `gmtTimeTool` tool will be to act as an API that can say the current time for a given location.

To simulate the unreliability of real-world scenarios, we randomly introduce failures for every third call.

The tools' implementations are just mockups. In production, static strings such as `The local time in ${city} is 6:30pm.` will be replaced with actual API calls.

We define the schema for the tool using the `zod` library:

```
const gmtTimeSchema = z.object({
  city: z.string().describe("The name of the city"),
})

const gmtTimeTool = tool(
  async ({ city }) => {
    const serviceIsWorking = Math.floor(Math.random() * 3)
    return serviceIsWorking !== 2
```

```
        ? `The local time in ${city} is 6:30pm.`
        : "Error 404"
  },
  {
     name: "gmtTime",
     description: "Check local time in a specified city."
       + " The API is randomly available every third call.",
     schema: gmtTimeSchema,
  }
)


const toolNode = new ToolNode([gmtTimeTool])
```

One of the roles of an AI agent is to decide what tools to use to get the job done. In this case, the decision will be quite simple, given that we provided the Agent with just one single tool.

Don't worry, we will go into much more detail on how tools are working in the next chapter.

4.4. Defining the Agent's Graph with LangGraph.js

The AI agent's graph defines how the conversation flows between nodes, or stages, of the conversation. It sets up nodes for invoking the LLM and tool usage, and defines how to switch between them:

```
const graph = new StateGraph(MessagesAnnotation)
  .addNode("agent", callModelNode)
  .addNode("tools", toolNode)
  .addEdge(START, "agent")
  .addEdge("tools", "agent")
  .addConditionalEdges("agent", shouldContinue, ["tools", END])

const runnable = graph.compile()
```

Here, `addNode()` links the steps in the AI's process, such as interacting with the `callModelNode` and the `toolNode`.

The `addConditionalEdges()` method ensures the workflow moves forward based on the result of the tool called.

In a later chapter, we will discuss the details of how the StateGraph works. For now, let's say it enables the AI agent to retain memory.

The structure of our Graph looks like so:

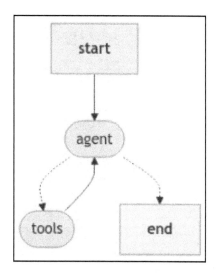

Remember that you can see the structure of the graph by running the following code:

```
const image = await runnable.getGraph().drawMermaidPng()
const arrayBuffer = await image.arrayBuffer()
await fs.writeFileSync(
  "graph-struct.png",
  new Uint8Array(arrayBuffer)
)
```

4.5. Setting Nodes in LangGraph

While the general workflow is defined using a graph object from LangGraph, we also need to define the content of each node of this graph.

The `shouldContinue()` function is the key component. It determines whether to continue or end the agent execution.

```
const callModelNode = async (state) => {
  const { messages } = state
  const llmWithTools = llm.bindTools([gmtTimeTool])
  const result = await llmWithTools.invoke(messages)
  return { messages: [result] }
}

const shouldContinue = (state) => {
  const lastMessage = getLastMessage(state)
  const didAICalledAnyTools = lastMessage._getType() === "ai" &&
    lastMessage.tool_calls?.length
  return didAICalledAnyTools ? "tools" : END
}
```

In this concrete example, the AI agent will have to decide when it has reached its objective, meaning that the API call to `gmtTime` successfully returned a valid response.

For example in the case where the API call fails we will see a stream of messages similar to the one below:

```
messages: [
  HumanMessage {
      "content": "What is the time now in Singapore? I would
        + " like to call a friend there."
      // more attributes here
```

```
    },
    ToolMessage {
        "content": "Error 404",
        "name": "gmtTime",
        // more attributes here
    },
    AIMessage {
        "content": "It seems there was an issue retrieving the "
          + " current time in Singapore. Let me try again.",
        // more attributes here
    },
      // keeps going until it receives an answer
]
```

4.6. Setting Up the AI agent Behavior

Now, we can feed in the messages and invoke the workflow. We set the scene for our AI agent by defining its responsibilities in a system message and then asking it to provide help for making a phone call:

```
const result = await runnable.invoke({
  messages: [
    new SystemMessage("You are responsible for answering user"
      + " questions using tools. These tools sometimes fail,"
      + " but you keep trying until you get a valid response."),
    new HumanMessage( "What is the time now in Singapore?"
      + " I would like to call a friend who lives there.")
  ]
})
```

Finally, we log the AI's response to the console:

```
console.log("AI:   " + getLastMessage(result).content )
```

We will get an output like the one below:

```
"AI: The current time in Singapore is 6:30 PM. You can call your
friend!"
```

One interesting fact about having AI features is that if we change the output of the `gmtTimeTool` the model will know how to interpret the response and make recommendations:

```
// updating the output of gmtTimeTool
return `The local time in ${city} is 1:15am.`

// will lead to updating the final output
"AI: Current time in Singapore is 1:15AM. Might be early for a
phone call."
```

4.7. Putting It All Together

To get an overview of the complete flow, this is how the final version of the code will look like:

```
import { HumanMessage, SystemMessage } from
"@langchain/core/messages"
import { ToolNode } from "@langchain/langgraph/prebuilt"
import {
  END, MessagesAnnotation, START, StateGraph
} from "@langchain/langgraph"
import { ChatOpenAI } from "@langchain/openai"
import { tool } from "@langchain/core/tools"
import { z } from "zod"
import * as dotenv from "dotenv"

dotenv.config({ path: '../.env' })

const llm = new ChatOpenAI({ model: "gpt-4o", temperature: 0 })

const getLastMessage =
  ({ messages }) => messages[messages.length - 1]

const gmtTimeSchema = z.object({
  city: z.string().describe("The name of the city")
})

const gmtTimeTool = tool(
  async ({ city }) => {
    const serviceIsWorking = Math.floor(Math.random() * 3)
    return serviceIsWorking !== 2
      ? `The local time in ${city} is 6:30pm.`
      : "Error 404"
  },
```

```
{
    name: "gmtTime",
    description: "Check local time in a specified city. The API"
        + " fails randomly.",
    schema: gmtTimeSchema,
  }
)

const tools = [gmtTimeTool]
const toolNode = new ToolNode(tools)
const llmWithTools = llm.bindTools(tools)

const callModelNode = async (state) => {
  const { messages } = state
  const result = await llmWithTools.invoke(messages)
  return { messages: [result] }
}

const shouldContinue = (state) => {
  const lastMessage = getLastMessage(state)
  const didAICalledAnyTools = lastMessage._getType() === "ai" &&
    lastMessage.tool_calls?.length
  return didAICalledAnyTools ? "tools" : END
}

const graph = new StateGraph(MessagesAnnotation)
 .addNode("agent", callModelNode)
 .addNode("tools", toolNode)
 .addEdge(START, "agent")
 .addEdge("tools", "agent")
 .addConditionalEdges("agent", shouldContinue, ["tools", END])

const runnable = graph.compile()
```

```
const result = await runnable.invoke({
  messages: [
    new SystemMessage("You are responsible for answering user"
      + " questions using tools. These tools sometimes fail"
      + ", but you keep trying until you get a valid response."),
    new HumanMessage("What is the time now in Singapore?"
      + " I would like to call a friend who lives there.")
  ]
})

console.log("AI: " + getLastMessage(result).content)
```

The code we built here showcases a resilient agent that can handle failures and retry operations, simulating real-world scenarios where APIs might occasionally fail. This setup provides a foundation for more complex personal assistants with broader applications.

5. Tool Calling

5.1. Tool Calling and Functions

Tools are a crucial aspect in understanding how AI agents are built, and in this chapter we will explore how they work.

What is tool calling? Tool calling is a way to provide an LLM with a set of code functions and schemas. The LLM takes these functions as inputs and returns if it needs to use one or more code functions to answer a user's question.

Tool calling is often linked to function calling. A tool can be made of multiple functions.

Tools and functions are helpful if you want to provide the user with highly dynamic information that was not trained in the model.

Let's take an example. A user wants to go for a hike on the weekend in a specific city and book a room in a hotel for an overnight stay.

This is how the initial prompt for the LLM will look:

```
"How will the weather be in Valencia this weekend?  I would like
to go for a weekend-long hike and book one  room for Saturday
night."
```

To answer the above request, the tools for the following API calls:

1. `weatherApi(city)` - checks if the weather is suitable for a hike in a given city;
2. `hotelsAvailability(city)` - checks if any hotel rooms are available in a city.

5.2. Tool Calling Does Not Invoke the Actual Function

The name "tool calling" implies that the LLM performs some action on its own, but that's not the case. This is a common source of confusion.

The LLM only suggests the function names and the arguments that function should use when invoked. It's up to us to run the functions with the suggested arguments.

In the above example, the result of tool calling means that the LLM will decide that it needs to call the following:

```
[
  {
    functionName: 'weatherApi',
    parameters: [{
      name: 'city',
      value: 'Valencia'
    }]
  },
  {
    functionName: 'hotelsAvailability',
    parameters: [{
      name: 'city',
      value: 'Valencia'
    }]
  }
]
```

However, in a non agentic system, the LLM will not make the actual call of these functions. It's up to the developer to invoke the functions requested by the LLM.

5.3. Tool Calling Support

Note that not all available LLMs support tool calling.

You can check out the table from
https://python.langchain.com/v0.2/docs/integrations/chat/ to see if a model can handle tool calls.

So, before trying to use tool calling, make sure your selected model supports this feature.

Next, let's go through a full code example of using Tool Calling with LangChain.

In the second part, we will see how to implement and use tool calling with LangChain.

Note that tool calling is only available from `@langchain/core` version 0.2.7 and above. You can find the official documentation
https://js.langchain.com/v0.2/docs/how_to/tool_calling/.

Let's get to work!

5.4. Use Case Description

The use case of our example is to create an AI assistant that can help the user with a request similar to the following:

```
"How will the weather be in Valencia this weekend? I would like to
go for a weekend-long hike and book one room for Saturday."
```

If we run this prompt as it is, we will get this response from the LLM:

```
"I'm sorry, but I am unable to provide real-time weather updates.
I recommend checking a reliable weather website or app for the
most up-to-date information on the weather in Valencia this
weekend. Additionally, I suggest booking a room in advance to
ensure availability  for your weekend hike. Enjoy your trip!"
```

It's clear that the model does not have all the data, so we need to provide it with tools to retrieve this information.

5.5. Defining Schemas and Tools

To answer the above request, our LLM will need 2 tools:

1. One tool to retrieve weather data for a city.

2. Another tool to check if rooms are available in a city for a given day.

The first thing we need to do is define schemas for the tools. At this moment, the schema will only contain the parameters used by the tool functions and their descriptions.

The Zod schema library is perfect for this task.

```
import { z } from "zod"

const weatherApiSchema = z.object({
  city: z.string().describe("The name of the city")
})

const hotelsAvailabilitySchema = z.object({
  city: z.string().describe("The name of the city"),
  day: z.string().describe("Day of the week to book the hotel"),
})
```

Remember that later on the LLM will use these description to determine what values should be assigned to the parameters.

Based on these schemas, we can define the tools and pass them to the LLM:

```
import { tool } from "@langchain/core/tools"
import { ChatOpenAI } from "@langchain/openai"

const llm = new ChatOpenAI({ temperature: 0 })
```

```
const weatherApiTool = tool(
  async ({ city }) => {
    return `The weather in ${city} is sunny, 20°C`
  },
  {
    name: "weatherApi",
    description: "Check the weather in a specified city.",
    schema: weatherApiSchema,
  }
)

const hotelsAvailabilityTool = tool(
  async ({ city, day }) => {
    return `Hotel rooms in ${city} are available for ${day}.`
  },
  {
    name: "hotelsAvailability",
    description: "Check if hotels are available in a given city.",
    schema: hotelsAvailabilitySchema,
  }
)

const llmWithTools = llm.bindTools([
  weatherApiTool,
  hotelsAvailabilityTool
])
```

Some things to notice here:

- Descriptions are crucial, as they will be passed along to the model along with the function name.

- Functions must return strings.

- The tools' implementations are just mockups. In production, static strings such as "The weather in ${city} is sunny, 20°C" will be replaced with actual API calls.

- Remember that not all models support tool calling. Be sure to use a model that supports this feature.

5.6. Invoking the Tools, the Tool Calls & Finish Reason Fields, and the ToolMessage Class

Having these tools defined, if we invoke the model, we will see that it will not return anything:

```
let llmOutput = await llmWithTools.invoke("How will the weather"
  + " be in Valencia this weekend? I would like to go for a"
  + " weekend-long hike and book one room for Saturday.")
console.log(llmOutput)

// WAIT: the llmOutput.content is empty
// "content": ""
```

The LLM is not calling the actual tool. The LLM only suggests the function names and the arguments that the function should use when invoked. It's up to us to run the functions with the suggested arguments.

We need to check if the `response_metadata.finish_reason` field is set to the `tool_calls` value. If so, it's up to us to go through the `tool_calls` array and invoke the tools.

In this particular case, the `tool_calls[]` array will contain the following values:

```
"tool_calls": [
  {
    "name": "weatherApi",
    "args": {
      "city": "Valencia"
    },
    "type": "tool_call",
    "id": "call_wLNjQ1MdekA2YSzFyANSQdBt"
```

```
  },
  {
    "name": "hotelsAvailability",
    "args": {
      "city": "Valencia",
      "day": "Saturday"
    },
    "type": "tool_call",
    "id": "call_yY5ZAFKwcMGqRFM4RGgSGkj2"
  }
]
```

These tools need to be called manually, and the values for `args` need to be passed in as parameters:

```
let toolMapping = {
  "weatherApi": weatherApiTool,
  "hotelsAvailability": hotelsAvailabilityTool
}

for await (let toolCall of llmOutput.tool_calls) {
  let tool = toolMapping[toolCall["name"]]
  let toolOutput = await tool.invoke(toolCall.args)
  let newTM = new ToolMessage({
    tool_call_id: toolCall.id,
    content: toolOutput
  })
  messages.push(newTM)
}

llmOutput = await llmWithTools.invoke(messages)

console.log(llmOutput)
```

An easy way to integrate the info returned by a tool, is to package it with using the `@langchain/core/messages/ToolMessage` utility class.

If we take a look at the code for the `@langchain/core/tools/tool` class, we will see it implements the `Runnable` interface; therefore, it supports the standard LCEL calling via the `invoke()` function.

5.7. Putting It All Together

This is what a full example may look like:

```javascript
import { tool } from "@langchain/core/tools"
import { z } from "zod"
import { ChatOpenAI } from "@langchain/openai"
import { HumanMessage, ToolMessage } from
"@langchain/core/messages"
import * as dotenv from "dotenv"

dotenv.config({ path: '../.env' })
const llm = new ChatOpenAI({ temperature: 0 })

const weatherApiSchema = z.object({
  city: z.string().describe("The name of the city")
})

const weatherApiTool = tool(
  async ({ city }) => {
    return `The weather in ${city} is sunny, 20°C`
  },
  {
    name: "weatherApi",
    description: "Check the weather in a specified city.",
    schema: weatherApiSchema,
  }
)

const hotelsAvailabilitySchema = z.object({
  city: z.string().describe("The name of the city"),
  day: z.string().describe("Day of the week to book the hotel"),
})
```

```javascript
const hotelsAvailabilityTool = tool(
  async ({ city, day }) => {
    return `Hotel rooms in ${city} are available for ${day}.`
  },
  {
    name: "hotelsAvailability",
    description: "Check if hotels are available in a given city.",
    schema: hotelsAvailabilitySchema,
  }
)

const llmWithTools = llm.bindTools([
  weatherApiTool,
  hotelsAvailabilityTool
])

let messages = [
  new HumanMessage("How's the weather in Valencia this weekend?"
    + " I would like to go for a weekend hike and book one room"
    + " for Saturday.")
]

let llmOutput = await llmWithTools.invoke(messages)
messages.push(llmOutput)

let toolMapping = {
  "weatherApi": weatherApiTool,
  "hotelsAvailability": hotelsAvailabilityTool
}

for await (let toolCall of llmOutput.tool_calls) {
  let tool = toolMapping[toolCall["name"]]
  let toolOutput = await tool.invoke(toolCall.args)
  let newTM = new ToolMessage({
```

```
      tool_call_id: toolCall.id,
      content: toolOutput
    })
    messages.push(newTM)
  }

  llmOutput = await llmWithTools.invoke(messages)

  console.log(llmOutput)
```

At this point, the `response_metadata.finish_reason` field will be set to `stop`, and the `content` property of the response will look like this:

```
"The weather in Valencia this weekend will be sunny with a
temperature of 20°C. Hotel rooms in Valencia are available for
Saturday, so you can book a room for your weekend hike."
```

As a test, we can update the response from the `weatherApiTool` to be `The weather in ${city} is heavy snow, -15°C`.

Now, if we run the example again, we will get:

```
"The weather in Valencia this weekend is heavy snow with a
temperature of -15°C. It may not be the best time to go for a hike.
Hotel rooms in Valencia are available for Saturday."
```

5.8. AI agents and Tools

AI agents are able to invoke these tools automatically.

We will not need to go through the `llmOutput.tool_calls` list and manually invoke the tools. The agent is able to make a plan to achieve it's objective and use the available tools to accomplish its objective.

Even if is was a long introduction I think it's important and productive to understand how all of these concepts work under the hood. The less "magic" involved in the process the more likely you are to get the expected outcome.

By the way, as a general rule, it's best to give the agent as few tools as possible.

6. Using Stateful Graphs

6.1. Introduction

You may have noticed in the previous examples that we have started using a new type of graph, the StateGraph:

```
import { StateGraph } from "@langchain/langgraph"
```

As the name implies, this graph type provides a state to the graph. The state can later be used to store and keep track of values across different nodes and cycles of the graph.

Let's take another look at the components that power an AI agent:

Since LLMs are stateless, meaning they can't remember previous interactions, we need to provide the MEMORY component. This is where utilities like the StateGraph come into play.

In an earlier example, we built an AI agent that checks the local timezone of a given city to help us schedule a phone call:

```
"AI: The current time in Singapore is 6:30 PM. You can call your
friend!"
```

However, the GMT time Tool function failed 33% of the time:

```
messages: [
  HumanMessage {
```

```
        "content": "What is the time now in Singapore? I would"
            + " like to call a friend there.",
        // more attributes here
    },
    ToolMessage {
        "content": "Error 404",
        "name": "gmtTime",
        // more attributes here
    },
    AIMessage {
        "content": "It seems there was an issue retrieving the"
            + " current time in Singapore. Let me try again.",
        // more attributes here
    },
    // keeps going until it receives an answer
]
```

Since LLMs are stateless, meaning they can't remember previous interactions, how was the AI agent able to remember that the previous tool call failed and needed to try again?

Well, the answer lies in the following line:

```
const graph = new StateGraph(MessagesAnnotation)
```

Before diving into the underlying mechanisms of the MessagesAnnotation, we need to take a short detour to discuss channels and reducers.

Ultimately, MessagesAnnotation is a built-in annotation that handles stateful conversation messages as they flow through the graph.

Let's begin by exploring how to set up and work with basic state values in LangGraph using channels.

6.2. Using Channels Within StateGraph

At the core of a graph in LangGraph is the agent's state. This state is a mutable object used to track the information available to the agent as execution progresses through the graph.

For example, the code below will create a simple graph that tracks the number of actions taken:

```
import { END, START,
    StateGraph, Annotation } from "@langchain/langgraph"

const GraphAnnotation = Annotation.Root({
    // Define a 'steps' channel
    steps: Annotation({
      // Default function: Initialize the channel with the
      // default value
      default: () => 0,
      // Reducer function: updates the current state
      reducer: (currentState, newValue) => currentState + 1,
    })
})

const funcGreen = state => {
    console.log("function Green")
    console.log(state)
    return state
}

const funcYellow = state => {
    console.log("function Yellow")
    console.log(state)
    return state
}
```

```
// build the graph
const workflow = new StateGraph(GraphAnnotation)
    // nodes
    .addNode("nodeGreen", funcGreen)
    .addNode("nodeYellow", funcYellow)
    // edges
    .addEdge(START, "nodeGreen")
    .addEdge("nodeGreen", "nodeYellow")
    .addEdge("nodeYellow", END)

const graph = workflow.compile()

await graph.invoke({})
// calling default same as doing graph.invoke({ steps: 0 })
```

The architecture of the graph is straightforward; we simply move directly from one node to another:

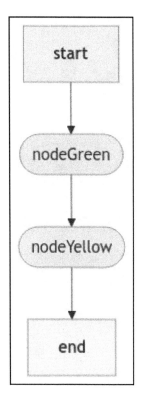

Running this code will produce the following output:

```
function Green
{ steps: 0 }
function Yellow
{ steps: 1 }
```

Each data is stored in a channel container defined using the Annotation class:

```
const GraphAnnotation = Annotation.Root({
    // Define a 'steps' channel
    steps: Annotation({
      // Default function: Initialize the channel with the
      // default value
      default: () => 0,
      // Reducer function: updates the current state
      reducer: (currentState, newValue) => currentState + 1,
    })
})
```

For a given channel, we can define a default function, which is called during initialization, along with an updater mechanism using a reducer function.

Once the state is added to the graph, it can be referenced and used in any node via the implicit state parameter:

```
const funcNode = state => {
    // do stuff with the state values
    return state
}
```

As we will see later, using state variables becomes a powerful tool for enabling human-in-the-loop validation.

6.3. Messages Annotation

In a graph's state, certain elements are commonly tracked, such as the conversation messages exchanged during execution.

This need is so common that there is a prebuilt annotation called MessagesAnnotation. This built-in annotation simplifies managing the channel where conversation messages are stored in the graph's state.

```
import { MessagesAnnotation, StateGraph } from
"@langchain/langgraph";


const graph = new StateGraph(MessagesAnnotation)
  .addNode(...)
  ...
```

This is equivalent to initializing your state manually like this:

```
import { BaseMessage } from "@langchain/core/messages";
import { Annotation, StateGraph,
  messagesStateReducer } from "@langchain/langgraph";

export const StateAnnotation = Annotation.Root({
  messages: Annotation({
    reducer: messagesStateReducer,
    default: () => [],
  }),
});

const graph = new StateGraph(StateAnnotation)
  .addNode(...)
  ...
```

The state of a MessagesAnnotation has a key called messages that can be used to reference the conversation history:

```
const callModelNode = async (state) => {
  const { messages } = state
  const result = await llmWithTools.invoke(messages)
  return { messages: [result] }
}
```

Alongside MessagesAnnotation, there are also other builtin annotations for common scenarios.

To wrap things up, using stateful graphs in LangGraph is like giving your AI agents a memory boost. With tools like StateGraph and MessagesAnnotation, you can easily keep track of what's happening as your agent moves through its tasks.

It's a straightforward way to make your workflows smarter and more responsive, opening the door to context aware possibilities.

7. Threads

7.1. Introduction

In the context of multiple users and topics, keeping track of what the AI agent knows and doesn't know can be a bit tricky.

Let's take the following example of an AI agent getting the following queue of requests:

```
{ user: 'Mike', msg: 'What is the sum of 2 and 4?' }
// 6
{ user: 'Bob', msg: 'Did England ever won the FIFA World Cup?' }
// yes
{ user: 'Mike', msg: 'Now, multily that by 10.' }
// 60
{ user: 'Bob', msg: 'When was that?' }
// 1966
```

In this example, the word "that" references two very different concepts:

1. the result of a math operation
2. the year when England won the football World Cup

Imagine talking to someone, but every time they forget what you just said. Or they confuse parts of your conversation with parts of conversations they had with others. Well, that's where LangGraph's threading system comes to the rescue.

In this chapter, we'll dive into how you can use threads to manage conversation persistence in LangGraph. This approach ensures that each thread has its own memory, making your interactions with AI agents more context-aware. Let's walk through this step by step.

7.2. Why Threads in LangGraph?

Think of threads like different lanes on a highway. Each lane, or thread, has its own flow of traffic, like a conversation. If you stay in one lane, you remember the cars that were there before. But if you switch lanes, you're in a new flow of traffic. In LangGraph, threads allow us to separate conversation contexts so that your interactions with AI agents don't get tangled up.

Take, for example, the conversation threads below:

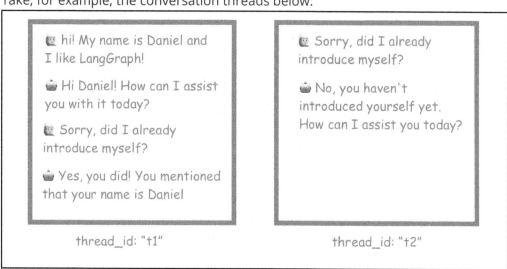

By using threads, we create isolated memory tracks that help the AI respond more accurately based on the specific conversation context.

7.3. Setting Up the LLM and the Graph

Before we jump into implementing threads, let's lay the foundation by setting up our LangGraph environment.

We're using the ChatOpenAI model, so let's ensure our configurations are ready:

```javascript
import { HumanMessage } from "@langchain/core/messages"
import {
  END, START, StateGraph, MessagesAnnotation, MemorySaver
} from "@langchain/langgraph"
import { ChatOpenAI } from "@langchain/openai"
import * as dotenv from "dotenv"

dotenv.config({ path: '../.env' })

const llm = new ChatOpenAI({
  model: "gpt-4o",
  temperature: 0,
})

const callModelNode = async (state) => {
  const { messages } = state
  const result = await llm.invoke(messages)
  return { messages: [result] }
}

const workflow = new StateGraph(MessagesAnnotation)
  .addNode("agent", callModelNode)
  .addEdge(START, "agent")
  .addEdge("agent", END)

// Initialize memory to persist state between graph runs
const checkpointer = new MemorySaver()
```

```
const graph = workflow.compile({ checkpointer });
```

This code sets up the environment to interact with the GPT-4 model.

To manage our conversation, we create a state graph that handles the flow of messages. This graph is simple, just taking the input and passing it to the LLM.

Note the checkpointer parameter. LangGraph uses checkpointers to save the graph state after each step.

One of the checkpointers is the builtin MemorySaver.

7.4. Introducing the Configurable Parameter and thread_id

Now comes the fun part—using threads to manage separate conversation contexts. We're going to simulate two different conversations and see how the AI handles each thread independently.

Once we have the checkpointer mechanism in place, we will need to specify a thead_id to store the different graph states. A thread is basicly a collection of saved checkpoints.

Let's start the first thread. In this thread, we'll introduce ourselves to the AI and see if it remembers us later.

```
console.log("Starting first thread")
const configIntroThread = {
  configurable: { thread_id: "t1" }
}


// First interaction: introducing ourselves
const t1r1 = await graph.invoke({
  messages: [
    new HumanMessage("hi! My name is Daniel and I like
LangGraph!")
],}, configIntroThread)
console.log(getLastMessage(t1r1).content)
// "Hi Daniel! How can I assist you with it today?"
```

The AI correctly acknowledges our introduction. Now, let's see if it remembers this introduction when we ask about it later in the same thread:

```
const t1r2 = await graph.invoke({
  messages: [
    new HumanMessage("Sorry, did I already introduce myself?")
],}, configIntroThread)
console.log(getLastMessage(t1r2).content)
// "Yes, you did! You mentioned that your name is Daniel
// and that you like LangGraph."
```

Success! The AI remembers our name because we're still in the same thread.

The key parts are the `thread_id` in the `configurable` parameter and the `checkpointer` defined in the previous step.

Starting a second thread. Let's switch to a new thread and ask the AI the same question. Will it remember us this time?

```
console.log("Starting second thread")
const configAnotherThread = {
  configurable: { thread_id: "t2" }
}


// Asking the same question in a new thread
const t2r1 = await graph.invoke({
  messages: [
    new HumanMessage("Sorry, did I already introduce myself?")
],}, configAnotherThread)
console.log(getLastMessage(t2r1).content)

// "No, you haven't introduced yourself yet.
// How can I assist you today?"
```

This time, the AI has no memory of our introduction. That's because we're in a different thread with its own isolated memory: `thread_id: "t2"`.

You can see threads like the multiple conversation panels in the web version of ChatGPT:

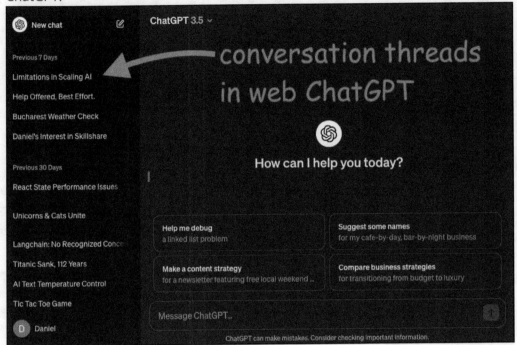

Using threads like this is essential when building applications that require managing multiple user contexts. Imagine a customer service bot handling different users simultaneously—each thread keeps track of the user's specific issue without mixing up conversations.

Threads ensure that the AI's memory is scoped to the conversation at hand.

7.5. Putting it All Together

Let's see how all of this looks in code:

```
import { HumanMessage } from "@langchain/core/messages"
import {
  END, START, StateGraph, MessagesAnnotation, MemorySaver
} from "@langchain/langgraph"
import { ChatOpenAI } from "@langchain/openai"
import * as dotenv from "dotenv"

dotenv.config({ path: '../.env' })

const llm = new ChatOpenAI({
  model: "gpt-4o",
  temperature: 0,
})

const getLastMessage = ({ messages }) =>
  messages[messages.length - 1]

const callModelNode = async (state) => {
  const { messages } = state
  const result = await llm.invoke(messages)
  return { messages: [result] }
}

const workflow = new StateGraph(MessagesAnnotation)
  .addNode("agent", callModelNode)
  .addEdge(START, "agent")
  .addEdge("agent", END)

// Initialize memory to persist state between graph runs
const checkpointer = new MemorySaver()
```

```javascript
const graph = workflow.compile({ checkpointer });

console.log("Starting first thread")
const configIntroThread = {
  configurable: { thread_id: "t1" }
}
// First, let's introduce ourselves to the AI
const t1r1 = await graph.invoke({
  messages: [
    new HumanMessage("hi! My name is Daniel and I like
LangGraph!")
],}, configIntroThread)
console.log(getLastMessage(t1r1))
/ Hi Daniel! How can I assist you with it today?

// Does the AI remember us?
const t1r2 = await graph.invoke({
  messages: [
    new HumanMessage("Sorry, did I already introduce myself?")
],}, configIntroThread)
console.log(getLastMessage(t1r2).content)
// Yes, you did! You mentioned that your name is Daniel
// and that you like LangGraph.

console.log("Starting second thread")
const configAnotherThread = {
  configurable: { thread_id: "t2" }
}
// This is a brand new thread with no prior knowledge
const t2r1 = await graph.invoke({
  messages: [
    new HumanMessage("Sorry, did I already introduce myself?")
],}, configAnotherThread)
console.log(getLastMessage(t2r1).content)
```

```
// No, you haven't introduced yourself yet.
// How can I assist you today?
```

As we delve deeper into AI agent based workflows, managing conversation history using threads will be very useful.

As a general recap of the process:

- the checkpointer mechanism writes the state at every step of the graph
- these checkpoints are saved in a thread
- we can access that thread in the future using the thread id

8. Human in the Loop

8.1. What is Human in the Loop?

When discussing AI agents, one concept we can't overlook is Human in the Loop (HITL).

Human in the Loop refers to the active involvement of humans in the decision-making processes of AI agents. This ensures that AI actions are not entirely autonomous, especially in high-stakes scenarios.

Consider the following examples:

1. medical diagnosis: an AI suggests a diagnosis based on symptoms, but a doctor reviews the result to ensure accuracy before treatment begins.

2. financial transactions: an AI agent recommends transferring funds or making a high-value purchase, but a human confirms the transaction to avoid errors or fraud.

3. autonomous vehicles: a self-driving car makes driving decisions, but a human driver can take control if the AI encounters an unexpected situation or risk.

4. content creation: an AI agent assists in generating a marketing video. A human provides continuous feedback, adjusting the style, color, and message at each stage, refining the final product until it's perfect.

Each of these situations shows why it's sometimes necessary to merge the flow of an agent with a human operator.

8.2. Types of Human in the Loop Interactions

There are several ways to integrate humans into the AI loop. Let's explore some of them.

One common method is authorization. The AI agent requires human approval for specific actions before proceeding. For instance, an AI managing finances may suggest reimbursing a client or making a purchase, but a human must approve the final decision. This approach ensures safety and validates actions before execution.

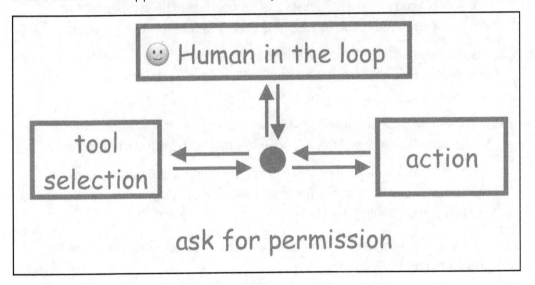

However, Human in the Loop can go beyond just authorization. Another key interaction type is continuous feedback loops, where humans provide guidance throughout the AI's work, not just at the end.

For example, if you're working with an autonomous coding agent like Devin AI, and you ask it to "Make me a clone of Twitter," you could end up waiting hours for an output that doesn't meet your expectations.

With continuous feedback, you don't wait passively. Instead, you review the AI's progress at various stages, refining its output step by step. You might direct the agent by saying, "Make the feed layout similar to Twitter's home page," or "Ensure the app scales for mobile users." This back-and-forth process helps ensure the final result aligns with your needs.

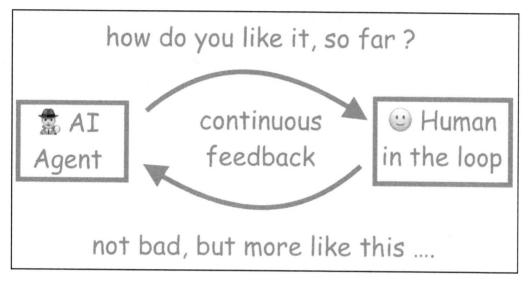

This approach is much more efficient, especially for tasks where the final result is subjective or complex.

8.3. Example Setup

A common HITL interaction pattern involves the AI agent pausing to request human input, allowing for clarification and feedback. In LangGraph, this dynamic is implemented through well placed breakpoints that halt graph execution at critical points. During these pauses, the agent waits for user input, integrates the feedback into the graph state, and then smoothly resumes execution.

Let's say we want to create an AI agent that helps with travel planning.

The structure of the agent is quite straightforward. It will use a purchase ticket tool to buy plane tickets.

This is the initial state of the application:

```
import {
    END,
    START,
    StateGraph,
    MessagesAnnotation
} from "@langchain/langgraph"
import { ChatOpenAI } from "@langchain/openai"
import { HumanMessage } from "@langchain/core/messages"
import { z } from "zod"
import { tool } from "@langchain/core/tools"
import * as dotenv from "dotenv"

dotenv.config({ path: '../.env' })

const llm = new ChatOpenAI({
    model: "gpt-4o",
    temperature: 0,
})

const purchaseTicketTool = tool(
```

```
        (input) => "Successfully purchased a plane ticket for " +
            + input.destination,
        {
            name: "purchase_ticket",
            description: "Buy a plane ticket for a given
destination.",
            schema: z.object({
                destination: z.string().describe("The destination of
the plane ticket."),
            }),
        }
    )

const tools = [purchaseTicketTool]

const nodeTools = async (state) => {
    const { messages } = state
    const lastMessage = messages[messages.length - 1]
    const toolCall = lastMessage.tool_calls[0]
    // invoke the tool to buy the plane ticket
    const result = await purchaseTicketTool.invoke(toolCall)
    return { messages: result }
}

const nodeAgent = async (state) => {
    const { messages } = state
    const llmWithTools = llm.bindTools(tools)
    const result = await llmWithTools.invoke(messages)
    return { messages: [result] }
}

const shouldContinue = (state) => {
    const { messages } = state
    const lastMessage = messages[messages.length - 1]
```

```
    if (lastMessage._getType() !== "ai" ||
!lastMessage.tool_calls?.length) {
        // LLM did not call any tools,
        // or not AI message, so we have to end
        return END
    }
    // tools are provided, so we should continue.
    return "tools"
}


const workflow = new StateGraph(MessagesAnnotation)
    .addNode("agent", nodeAgent)
    .addEdge(START, "agent")
    .addNode("tools", nodeTools)
    .addEdge("tools", "agent")
    .addConditionalEdges("agent", shouldContinue, ["tools", END])

const graph = workflow.compile()

const config = {
    configurable: { thread_id: "vacation" }
}
```

While we want the agent to be able to respond with information and use other tools, it should require human confirmation before using the purchase ticket tool.

At this moment, if we ask the agent to purchase a ticket, it will do so without any problem:

```
const config = {
    configurable: { thread_id: "vacation" }
}
```

```
const input = {
    messages: [
        new HumanMessage("Can I get a plane ticket to destination
New York?")
    ]
}

const result = await graph.invoke(input, config)

console.log(result)

// Successfully purchased a plane ticket for New York
```

Let's see how we can add a Human-in-the-Loop mechanism to prevent the unauthorized use of the purchase ticket tool.

8.4. LangGraph and HITL

LangGraph provides out of the box support for the Human-in-the-Loop (HITL) mechanism.

To add HITL for a given AI agent made with LangGraph, we need to do the following:

1. define the graph state variables to manage permissions.

2. set up the graph interruption checks.

3. break the flow when a specific event happens.

4. get human feedback.

5. update the graph state.

6. resume the flow.

The diagram below summarizes this process:

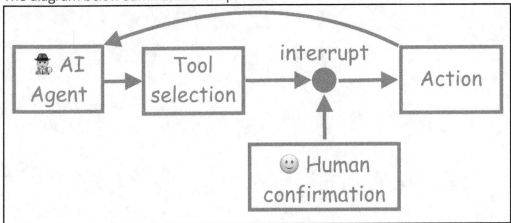

In the next chapters we will see how this gets translated into code.

8.5. Adding interruptions to the graph

The first step is to ensure we can stop the execution of the graph when it tries to use tools.

We will add interruptions to the workflow and throw an error if a condition is not met.

Here are the changes we will make:

```
// ...

// Add state variables
const graphState = Annotation.Root({
    ...MessagesAnnotation.spec,
    // Whether or not permission has been granted
    // to use the credit card
    askHumanUseCreditCard: Annotation(),
})

const nodeTools = async (state) => {
    const { messages, askHumanUseCreditCard } = state
    // Throw an error if the askHumanUseCreditCard
    // authorization is not met
    if (!askHumanUseCreditCard) {
        throw new Error("Permission to use credit card is
required.")
    }
    // ...
}

// ...

// Define checkpointers and set up interruption checks
```

```
const graph = workflow.compile({
    checkpointer: new MemorySaver(),
})

const config = {
    configurable: { thread_id: "vacation" },
    interruptBefore: ["tools"]
}

// ...
```

If we run the example with these changes in place, we will see that the agent is now attempting to use the tool, but only defines the arguments for the function. It does not make the actual function call.

```
const input = {
    messages: [
        new HumanMessage("Can I get a plane ticket to New York?")
    ]
}

console.log(await graph.invoke(input, config))

// "tool_calls": [{
//      "name": "purchase_ticket",
//      "args": {
//          "destination": "New York"
//      }]
```

8.6. Managing Permissions in the Graph State and Resuming the Flow

Now, let's see how we can manage human permissions and resume the flow of the graph.

At this moment, if we check the HITL state flag, we will get a value of `false`.

```
await graph.getState(config).values.askHumanUseCreditCard
```

We want to ask the user to type `yes` before the AI agent can make a real purchase.

To get keyboard input from the console, we need to install the `readline` library from NPM:

```
npm i readline-sync
```

We can now read the confirmation, update the graph state, and resume the flow:

```
const input = {
    messages: [
        new HumanMessage("Can I get a plane ticket to New York?")
    ]
}

const intermediaryResult = await graph.invoke(input, config)

console.log("WAIT: We need human authorization for this
operation.")

// Get human authorization
let userInput = reader.question("Type yes to allow credit card
use: ")
```

```
await graph.updateState(config, {
    askHumanUseCreditCard: userInput === "yes"
})


// Continue graph after state update
const finalResult = await graph.invoke(null, config)
console.log(finalResult)
```

Notice the `null` input for the second call of `graph.invoke(null, config)` after the state is updated.

With this setup, our workflow will proceed as follows:

```
// HITL authorization approved
`WAIT: We need human authorization for this operation.
Type yes to allow credit card use: yes
Successfully purchased a plane ticket to New York.
Your plane ticket to New York has been successfully purchased.
Safe travels!`

// Deny the HITL authorization
`WAIT: We need human authorization for this operation.
Type yes to allow credit card use: no
// throw new Error("Permission to use credit card is required.")`
```

8.7. Putting It All Together

And there you have it. This is how we can get the LangGraph agent to wait and react based on the human in the loop mechanism.

Below is the full code of the working example:

```javascript
import { END, START, StateGraph, MemorySaver,
    MessagesAnnotation, Annotation } from "@langchain/langgraph"
import { ChatOpenAI } from "@langchain/openai"
import { HumanMessage } from "@langchain/core/messages"
import { z } from "zod"
import { tool } from "@langchain/core/tools"
import * as dotenv from "dotenv"
import * as reader  from "readline-sync"


dotenv.config({ path: '../.env' })


const llm = new ChatOpenAI({
    model: "gpt-4o",
    temperature: 0,
})


const graphState = Annotation.Root({
    ...MessagesAnnotation.spec,
    // whether or not permission has been granted
    // to use credit card
    askHumanUseCreditCard: Annotation(),
})


const purchaseTicketTool = tool(
    (input) => `Successfully purchased a plane
    ticket for ${input.destination}`,
    {
```

```
        name: "purchase_ticket",
        description: "Buy a plane ticket for a given
destination.",
        schema: z.object({
            destination: z.string().describe("The destination of
the plane ticket."),
        }),
    }
)

const tools = [purchaseTicketTool]

const nodeTools = async (state) => {
    const { messages, askHumanUseCreditCard } = state
    if (!askHumanUseCreditCard) {
        throw new Error("Permission to use credit card is
required.")
    }
    const lastMessage = messages[messages.length - 1]
    const toolCall = lastMessage.tool_calls[0]
    // invoke the tool to buy the plane ticket
    const result = await purchaseTicketTool.invoke(toolCall)
    return { messages: result }
}

const nodeAgent = async (state) => {
    const { messages } = state
    const llmWithTools = llm.bindTools(tools)
    const result = await llmWithTools.invoke(messages)
    return { messages: [result] }
}

const shouldContinue = (state) => {
    const { messages } = state
```

```
    const lastMessage = messages[messages.length - 1]
    if (lastMessage._getType() !== "ai" ||
!lastMessage.tool_calls?.length) {
        // LLM did not call any tools,
        // or not AI message, so we have to end
        return END
    }
    // tools are provided, so we should continue.
    return "tools"
}

const workflow = new StateGraph(graphState)
    .addNode("agent", nodeAgent)
    .addEdge(START, "agent")
    .addNode("tools", nodeTools)
    .addEdge("tools", "agent")
    .addConditionalEdges("agent", shouldContinue, ["tools", END])

const graph = workflow.compile({
    checkpointer: new MemorySaver(),
})

const config = {
    configurable: { thread_id: "vacation" },
    interruptBefore: ["tools"]
}

const input = {
    messages: [
        new HumanMessage("Can I get a plane ticket to destination
New York?")
    ]
}
```

```
const intermediaryResult = await graph.invoke(input, config)

// mention await
graph.getState(config)).values.askHumanUseCreditCard

console.log("WAIT: We need human authorization for this
operation.")

// get human authorization
let userInput = reader.question("Type yes to allow credit card
use: ")
await graph.updateState(config, {
    askHumanUseCreditCard: userInput === "yes"
})

// continuing graph after state update
const finalResult = await graph.invoke(null, config)
console.log(finalResult)
```

As a fun exercise you can try adding a second tool to the AI agent named
`cityWeatherTool()`. You should use HITL only for the initial
`purchaseTicketTool()`.

9. Multi Agent Systems

9.1. Introduction

Now that we've seen the essentials of building AI agents with LangGraph let's dive into creating and managing a team of agents.

That's right! Multiple agents working together, each with their own goals and tools, all collaborating to achieve a shared objective.

But why use multiple specialized agents instead of one general-purpose agent?

The key is reliability. The more straightforward and clearly defined an agent's responsibilities, the more dependable it becomes. A study conducted by the LangChain team on using AI agents in production highlighted reliability as the most significant challenge: www.langchain.com/stateofaiagents.

Beyond reliability, there are several other compelling benefits to employing teams of specialized agents:

- flexibility; each agent can leverage different models tailored to unique tasks and capabilities

- speed and cost efficiency: specialized agents are optimized for their specific functions, reducing overhead

- simplified debugging: troubleshooting becomes much easier when issues can be isolated within smaller, focused sub-parts of the system

By splitting tasks among specialized agents, we get a more intelligent, faster, and more reliable way to build cool AI systems.

If interested, you can read more about this in the paper AutoGen Enabling Next-Gen LLM Applications via Multi-Agent Conversation: https://arxiv.org/abs/2308.08155.

9.2. What are we going to build

During this chapter, we will build a team of AI agents that will work together to help the user to conduct online research.

The team of agents is made of:

- the Researcher agent: it can go online and search the web using the Tavily API
- the Graph Generator agent: it renders data in a chart using simple characters

For a given task, we can use one single agent, or both.

This very small team of agents will be managed by a third agent named the Supervisor. The role of this agent will be to invoke one of the other 2 agents.

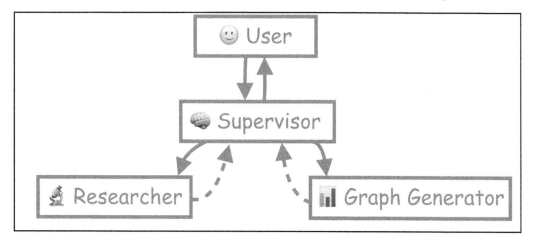

This is how an output sample of this multi-agent agent system will look like:

```
USER PROMPT: What was the GDP of Italy, Japan, and Mexico in 2023?


--------------------------
ITA (2255) | **********
JAP (4213) | *******************
MEX (1789) | ********
--------------------------
```

```
Here is the bar chart representing the GDP of Italy, Japan, and
Mexico in 2023:
- **Italy**: $2,254.85 billion USD
- **Japan**: $4,212.95 billion USD
- **Mexico**: $1,788.89 billion USD

This chart helps to compare the economic output of these countries
for that year.
```

For this particular case, both the Researcher agent and the Graph Generator agent were used to build the final output. However, there are cases that can be solved by only one single agent.

Also, remember that the data presented in the chart were scraped from the web, not taken from the training data for the LLM.

This is the file structure of our code:

```
/multi-agent
 ├── /etc
 │    ├── utils.js
 ├── /agents
 │    ├── chartGenerator.js
 │    ├── researcher.js
 │    ├── supervisor.js
 ├── .env
 ├── index.js
 ├── package-lock.json
 └── package.json
```

Each code sample will have a starting comment with the file location.

Let's get to work!

9.3. Building the Researcher Agent

One of the agents that will be part of our team will be the Researcher agent.

The scope of this agent is to use the Tavily search to perform online research.

Tavily is a search engine tailored for AI agents. This tool will allow our AI agents to do real-time, accurate search results tailored for LLMs and RAG.

The first thing we need to do is to generate an API Key for Tavily. You can do that by going to https://app.tavily.com/home, and after you sign in, you can get a free API key from the "API Key" section.

Once the Tavily API Key is generated, be sure to add it to the .env file:

```
OPENAI_API_KEY= your_key_here
TAVILY_API_KEY = your_key_here
```

Before getting started, we will create a utility file where we will place the common parts across all files:

```js
// FILE: etc/utils.js

import * as dotenv from "dotenv"
import { ChatOpenAI } from "@langchain/openai"

dotenv.config({ path: '../.env' })

const getLastMessage = ({ messages }) => messages[messages.length - 1]

const buildLLM = () => (new ChatOpenAI({
    modelName: "gpt-4o",
    temperature: 0
}))
```

```
export { getLastMessage, buildLLM }
```

We can build up the actual researcher tool once we have taken care of the utils file and the Tavily API key.

It will use a simple ReACT architecture, similar to the ones in the previous examples:

```
// FILE: agents/researcher.js

import { getLastMessage, buildLLM } from "../etc/utils.js"
import { TavilySearchResults } from
"@langchain/community/tools/tavily_search"
import { SystemMessage } from "@langchain/core/messages"
import { END, START, Annotation, messagesStateReducer,
    StateGraph } from "@langchain/langgraph"
import { ToolNode } from "@langchain/langgraph/prebuilt"


const llm = buildLLM()

const researcherAnnotation = Annotation.Root({
  messages: Annotation({
    reducer: messagesStateReducer,
    default: () => [
        new SystemMessage("You are a web researcher. You may"
            + " use the Tavily search engine to search the web"
            + " for important information, so the Chart Generator"
            + " in your team can make useful plots.")
    ]
  })
})


const tavilyTool = new TavilySearchResults()
```

```javascript
const tools = [tavilyTool]
const toolNode = new ToolNode(tools)

const callModel = async (state) => {
    const { messages } = state
    const result = await llm.bindTools(tools).invoke(messages)
    return { messages: [result] }
}

const shouldContinue = (state) => {
    const lastMessage = getLastMessage(state)
    const didAICalledAnyTools = lastMessage._getType() === "ai" &&
        lastMessage.tool_calls?.length
    return didAICalledAnyTools ? "tools" : END
}

const researcherGraph = new StateGraph(researcherAnnotation)
    .addNode("agent", callModel)
    .addNode("tools", toolNode)
    .addEdge(START, "agent")
    .addEdge("tools", "agent")
    .addConditionalEdges("agent", shouldContinue, ["tools", END])

const researcherAgent = researcherGraph.compile()

export { researcherAgent }
```

Let's give the reseacher agent a test drive:

```javascript
import { researcherAgent } from "./agents/researcher.js"
import { HumanMessage } from "@langchain/core/messages"
const result = await researcherAgent.invoke({
    messages: [
        new HumanMessage({
```

```
            content: "What is the current exchange rate of
EUR/USD?"
        })
    ]
})
console.log(result)

// AIMessage {
// "id": "chatcmpl-AbTIx2LnP4QdJsuWVfm75b6GQYWY7",
// "content": "Current exchange rate for EUR/USD is 1.0564 USD."
// "additional_kwargs": {}
```

What's important to note here is the fact that the results given by the agent are
real time, based on an actual web search, and not from the model's initial training
data.

9.4. Building the Graph Generation Agent

The Graph Generation Agent will have a similar ReACT architecture but has a different goal.

As the name implies, this Graph Generation Agent will render elementary graphs into the console.

For example, if we pass to the agent a data like the one below:

```
{
    {label: 'Ben', val: 5},
    {label: 'Joe', val: 10},
    {label: 'Dan', val: 18},
}
```

We will have a chart like this one printed in the console:

```
---------------------------
BEN   (5)  | ******
JOE  (10)  | ************
DAN  (18)  | ********************
---------------------------
```

The added value by the LLM will consist of:

- knowing when to call this tool
- extracting and formatting the data from a general text

This is the code for the chart drawing tool:

```
const chartTool = new tool(
    async ({ data }) => {
        const SCALE = 20
```

```
        const firstThreeChars = s => (s+"    ").slice(0,
3).toUpperCase()
        const normalizeToScale = (v, max) => Math.ceil(v / max *
SCALE)
        const getMaxVal = data => Math.max(...data.map(d =>
d.val))
        const maxVal = getMaxVal(data)

        console.log("---------------------------")
        data.forEach(({ label, val }) => {
            let result = `${firstThreeChars(label)}
(${Math.ceil(val)}) |`
            let normalizedVal = normalizeToScale(val, maxVal)
            result  = result + String('*').repeat(normalizedVal)
            console.log(result)
        })
        console.log("---------------------------")
        return "Chart has been generated and displayed to"
          + " the user!"
    },
    {
      name: "generate_bar_chart",
      description: "Generates a bar chart from an array of "
        + " data points and displays it for the user.",
      schema: z.object({
          data: z
            .object({
              label: z.string(),
              val: z.number()
            })
            .array()
      })
    }
)
```

This tool will do the following:

- each item from the table will be labeled using only the first three characters
- the numerical values will normalized and rendered at the given scale so that they can fit into the chart
- draw the chart using simple ASCII characters

This is the rest of the agent's code:

```javascript
// FILE: agents/chartAgent.js
import { getLastMessage, buildLLM } from "../etc/utils.js"
import { ChatOpenAI } from "@langchain/openai"
import { END, START, StateGraph, Annotation,
    messagesStateReducer } from "@langchain/langgraph"
import { ToolNode } from "@langchain/langgraph/prebuilt"
import { tool } from "@langchain/core/tools"
import { SystemMessage } from "@langchain/core/messages"
import { z } from "zod"


// the above chartTool comes here


const llm = buildLLM()

const chartGeneratorAnnotation = Annotation.Root({
    messages: Annotation({
        reducer: messagesStateReducer,
        default: () => [
          new SystemMessage("You excel at generating bar charts."
             + " Use the researcher's information to generate"
             + " the charts.")
        ]
    })
})
```

```
const tools = [chartTool]
const toolNode = new ToolNode(tools)

const callModel = async (state) => {
    const { messages } = state
    const result = await llm.bindTools(tools).invoke(messages)
    return { messages: [result] }
}

const shouldContinue = (state) => {
    const lastMessage = getLastMessage(state)
    const didAICalledAnyTools = lastMessage._getType() === "ai" &&
        lastMessage.tool_calls?.length
    return didAICalledAnyTools ? "tools" : END
}

const chartGenGraph = new StateGraph(chartGeneratorAnnotation)
    .addNode("agent", callModel)
    .addNode("tools", toolNode)
    .addEdge(START, "agent")
    .addEdge("tools", "agent")
    .addConditionalEdges("agent", shouldContinue, ["tools", END])

const chartGenAgent = chartGenGraph.compile()


export { chartGenAgent }
```

Let's now take this AI agent for a test drive:

```
import { HumanMessage } from "@langchain/core/messages"
const result  = await chartGenAgent.invoke({
    messages: [
        new HumanMessage({
            content: "Make me a chart with the following data: "
                + " Canada has 200 points, USA has 250 points,"
                + " Spain was 150 points."
        })
    ]
})
console.log(result)
```

As said, part of the added value of the LLM consists of extracting and formatting the data from a general context.

This chart is far from ideal, but choosing this straightforward implementation was intentional, so we can focus mainly on the AI integration part. You can use a third-party library such as D3: https://d3js.org/ for more reliable and better-looking charts.

Next, let's dive into how to orchestrate multi-agent systems.

9.5. Orchestrating AI Agents

At this point, we have now created two individual AI agents, each specializing in different tasks:

- the Researcher agent focuses on conducting online research using the Tavily web search tool
- the Chart Generator agent, focusing on rendering data into simple charts

We can use just the Researcher agent and the Chart Generator for a given task, or they can work together to accomplish the given task.

Let's see some examples:

1. the user wants to know who Abraham Lincoln was - only the Researcher agent will be used
2. the user asks for a report on the most significant economies by GDP in 2023 - both agents will be used. The Researcher will search for the data, while the Chart Generator agent will render the data into a nice graph

While this separation of responsibilities will increase the overall reliability of our system, we will also need to add a layer that controls when each agent will be called.

There are multiple architectures to manage agents in a multi-agent system:

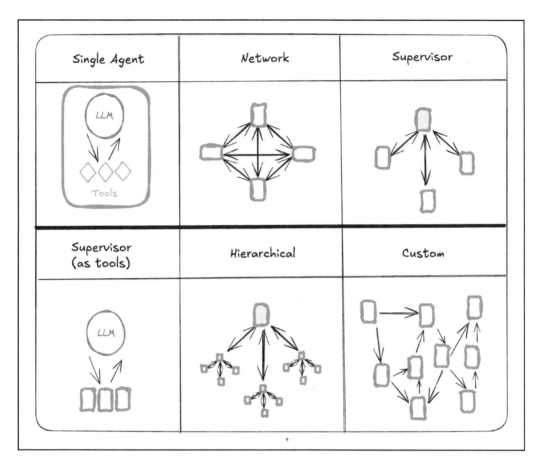

If you want to read more on this topic, a good place to start is this article from the official LangGraph documentation: https://langchain-ai.github.io/langgraph/concepts/multi_agent/

For our current example, we will use a supervisor agent.

9.6. Building the Supervisor Agent

We will first build a simple Supervisor agent in isolation. Its only scope is to take a prompt and indicate which agent from the team is a better fit to solve the task described in that prompt.

LangGraph works great with LangChain. For this particular agent, we will use some LangChain components in order to simplify the final code:

```js
// FILE: agents/supervisor.js

import { END } from "@langchain/langgraph"
import { z } from "zod"
import { JsonOutputToolsParser } from "langchain/output_parsers"
import { ChatPromptTemplate,
  MessagesPlaceholder } from "@langchain/core/prompts"
import { buildLLM } from "../etc/utils.js"


const llm = buildLLM()


const teamMembers = ["researcher", "chart_generator"]


const systemPrompt = "You are a supervisor tasked with managing"
  + " a conversation between the following workers:"
  + " {teamMembers}. Given the following user request, respond"
  + " with the worker to act next. Each worker will perform a"
  + " task and respond with their results and status. When"
  + " finished, respond with FINISH."


const options = [END, ...teamMembers]

const routingTool = {
  name: "route",
  description: "Select the next role.",
```

```
    schema: z.object({
      next: z.enum([END, ...teamMembers])
    })
  }

  const prompt = ChatPromptTemplate.fromMessages([
    ["system", systemPrompt],
    new MessagesPlaceholder("messages"),
    [
      "system",
      "Given the conversation above, who should act next?" +
      " Or should we FINISH? Select one of: {options}"
    ]
  ])

  const formattedPrompt = await prompt.partial({
    options: options.join(", "),
    teamMembers: teamMembers.join(", ")
  })

  const supervisor = formattedPrompt
    .pipe(llm.bindTools(
      [routingTool],
      { tool_choice: "route" }
    ))
    .pipe(new JsonOutputToolsParser())
    .pipe((x) => x[0].args)

  export { supervisor, teamMembers }
```

Let's take this Supervisor agent for a test drive. First, let's ask it to tell us the latest news about the stock market:

```
import { HumanMessage } from "@langchain/core/messages"
const response1  = await supervisor.invoke({
    messages: [
        new HumanMessage({
            content: "Tell me the latest news on the stock"
             + " market?"
 })
 ]
})
console.log(response1)


// { next: 'researcher' }
```

It will just reply with a JSON saying that the most suited Agent to complete this task is the Researcher.

Let's now ask another question. This time, we give it some clear data:

```
const response2  = await supervisor.invoke({
  messages: [
      new HumanMessage({
          content: "Mike is 41, Joe is 30. Give me a visual"
           + " representation of this data."
 })
 ]
})
console.log(response2)


// { next: 'chart_generator' }
```

If we have all the needed data, call the Chart Generator agent to build the graph.

Note that in the prompt, "Mike is 41, Joe is 30. Give me a visual representation of this data." we never mention graphs or charts! This is the beauty of LLMs. Not only will it know how to adapt to the context and invoke the correct function, but it will also know how to extract the data in an appropriate format:

```
const data = [
    {label: "Mike", age: 42},
    {label: "Joe", age: 30}
]
```

Even more, the Supervisor agent will know when to stop if the last received prompt indicates it:

```
import { HumanMessage } from "@langchain/core/messages"
const response3  = await supervisor.invoke({
    messages: [
        new HumanMessage({
            content: "all good"
  })
  ]
  })
console.log(response3)

// { next: '__end__' }
```

This will be very handy in ending the execution of the team of agents.

In the next part, we will plug this agent in as the main coordinator for our team of Agents.

9.7. Creating the Agents Team Graph

Now that we have the Supervisor agent ready, we can finally put all the pieces together.

Remember the interaction graph we have laid out at the beginning of this chapter:

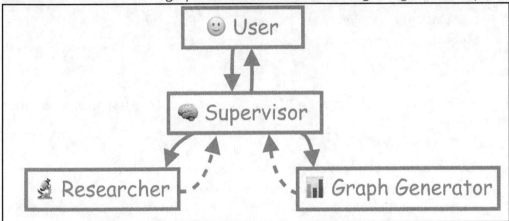

This graph will be defined in the main index file.

Let's take a look at the full code, and we will go into details right after.

This is the full code that manages the LangGraph team of AI agents:

```
// FILE: index.js

import { END, Annotation, START, StateGraph } from
"@langchain/langgraph"
import { HumanMessage } from "@langchain/core/messages"
import { getLastMessage } from "./etc/utils.js"
import { chartGenAgent, researcherAgent,
  supervisor, teamMembers } from "./agents/index.js"

const AgentState = Annotation.Root({
    messages: Annotation({
```

```
      reducer: (x, y) => x.concat(y),
      default: () => []
    }),
    next: Annotation({
      reducer: (x, y) => y ?? x ?? END,
      default: () => END
    })
})

const createAgentNode = (agent, nodeName) => async (state, config)
=> {
  const result = await agent.invoke(state, config)
  const { content } = getLastMessage(result)
  return {
    messages: [
      new HumanMessage({
        content,
        name: nodeName
      })
    ]
  }
}

const researcherNode = createAgentNode(researcherAgent,
"Researcher")
const chartGenNode = createAgentNode(chartGenAgent,
"ChartGenerator")

const workflow = new StateGraph(AgentState)
  .addNode("researcher", researcherNode)
  .addNode("chart_generator", chartGenNode)
  .addNode("supervisor", supervisor)
```

```
teamMembers.forEach((member) => workflow.addEdge(member,
"supervisor"))

workflow.addConditionalEdges("supervisor", (x) => x.next)

workflow.addEdge(START, "supervisor")

const graph = workflow.compile()
```

A few notes on the above code:

- the main annotation defines the object that is passed between each node of the main graph. Keep in mind that each agent has its own local annotation defined, such as the Researcher annotation or the Chart Generator annotation

- in this case, each graph node uses a previously defined agent. The Supervisor agent will make sure each is called for the appropriate task

- after an agent completes, it reports to the Supervisor.

With the graph created, we can finally invoke it and see how it performs!

Let's first ask the team a simple question that does not need a chart.

```
const result  = await graph.invoke({
    messages: [
        new HumanMessage({
            content: "Who was Abraham Lincoln?"
 })
 ]
})
console.log(result)

// will reply with something similar to:
// Abraham Lincoln was the 16th President of the United States,
// serving from ...
```

For this case, only the Researcher agent was used.

It's now time to see the full team in action:

```
const result  = await graph.invoke({
    messages: [
        new HumanMessage({
            content: "What are the top 3 winners of the"
             + " Fifa World Cup?"
 })
 ]
})
console.log(result)
```

We will get the following results:

```
--------------------------
BRA (5) | ********************
GER (4) | ****************
ITA (4) | ****************

--------------------------
Here are the top 3 top 3 FIFA World Cup winners by titles won.
```

For this request, the Supervisor agent decided we first needed more data. Therefore, the Researcher agent was called to action. After this, the Chart Generator could use the gathered data to build a visual representation.

9.8. Conclusion

We've built a reliable and adaptable multi-agent system by breaking down complex tasks into more smaller, more focused responsibilities.

Each agent serves a specific purpose, ensuring enhanced efficiency, better debugging, and cost-effectiveness. This modular approach simplifies the architecture and unlocks the potential for scaling as more tools and agents are added to the system.

10. ReACT AI Agents

10.1. Introduction

In this chapter, we'll explore the ReACT core agent architecture that forms the foundation of many flexible AI systems.

This architecture was introduced in the ReACT paper published in 2023 by Shunyu Yao from Princeton University and Google Research. You can read the full paper here: https://arxiv.org/abs/2210.03629.

ReACT merges verbal reasoning with task specific actions.

Traditionally, AI models focused on either reasoning (like Chain-of-Thought prompting) or action (like reinforcement learning). But rarely both. This separation led to key limitations: reasoning-heavy models often hallucinated facts, while action-based models lacked structured decision-making. ReACT solves this by forming a continuous feedback loop, where the agent reasons about the task, takes action, evaluates the results, and refines its next steps.

We have already seen the core structure of this architecture in the previous chapters:

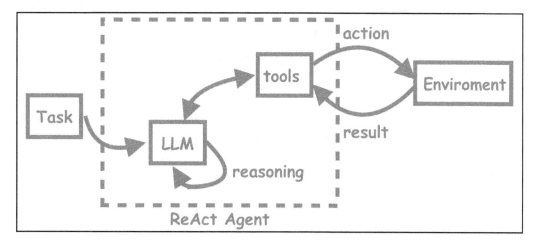

At the heart of ReACT lies a simple but powerful cycle: Reasoning, Acting (tool calling), and Responding.

Here's how it works:

- Reasoning: The agent thinks through the problem, breaking it down into logical steps.

- Acting (Tool Calling): The agent interacts with external tools, APIs, or databases to gather more information or execute actions.

- Responding: Based on the results, the agent updates its reasoning and decides the next step.

This cycle continues iteratively until the agent determines that no further actions are needed: Looping Until Completion.

This structured approach makes decision-making transparent, as the agent logs its thoughts, actions, and outcomes in a clear and explainable manner. Unlike "black-box" AI systems, ReACT agents explicitly log their thoughts, making it easy to track how decisions are made.

If an initial action doesn't yield the desired outcome, the agent loops back, adjusts its reasoning, and tries again. Rather than executing a single predetermined response, the agent evaluates multiple options before choosing the best course of action.

This architecture is ideal for complex problem-solving, such as research assistants, task automation, and multi-step workflows where adaptability is key.

10.2. Implementing the ReACT architecture from scratch

Let's see how we can implement an AI Agent that uses the ReACT architecture from scratch using LangGraph.

It will be a simple math AI Agent with two tools at its disposal:

- add: A JavaScript function to add two numbers.

- subtract: A JavaScript function to subtract two numbers.

```javascript
import { HumanMessage, SystemMessage } from
"@langchain/core/messages"
import { ToolNode } from "@langchain/langgraph/prebuilt"
import {
  END, MessagesAnnotation, START, StateGraph
} from "@langchain/langgraph"
import { ChatOpenAI } from "@langchain/openai"
import { z } from "zod"
import { tool } from "@langchain/core/tools"
import * as dotenv from "dotenv"


dotenv.config({ path: '../.env' })


const llm = new ChatOpenAI({ model: "gpt-4o", temperature: 0 })


const getLastMessage = ({ messages }) => messages[messages.length
- 1]


const addTool = tool(
    async ({ a, b }) => a + b,
  {
        name: "add",
        description: "Add two numbers together.",
```

```
        schema: z.object({
            a: z.number().describe("The first number"),
            b: z.number().describe("The second number")
 }),
 }
)


const subtractTool = tool(
  async ({ a, b }) => a - b,
 {
      name: "subtract",
      description: "Subtract two numbers.",
      schema: z.object({
          a: z.number().describe("The first number"),
          b: z.number().describe("The second number")
 }),
 }
)


const tools = [addTool, subtractTool]
const toolNode = new ToolNode(tools)
const llmWithTools = llm.bindTools(tools)


const callModel = async (state) => {
  const { messages } = state
  const result = await llmWithTools.invoke(messages)
  return { messages: [result] }
}


const shouldContinue = (state) => {
  const lastMessage = getLastMessage(state)
  const didAICallAnyTools = lastMessage._getType() === "ai" &&
    lastMessage.tool_calls?.length
  return didAICallAnyTools ? "tools" : END
```

```
}

const graph = new StateGraph(MessagesAnnotation)
 .addNode("agent", callModel)
 .addNode("tools", toolNode)
 .addEdge(START, "agent")
 .addEdge("tools", "agent")
 .addConditionalEdges("agent", shouldContinue, ["tools", END])

const runnable = graph.compile()
```

10.3. Using the createReactAgent() utility

The ReACT architecture is so commonly used that LangGraph provides a built-in
tool to create this type of agent:

```
import { createReactAgent } from "@langchain/langgraph/prebuilt"

const agent = createReactAgent({llm, tools})
```

We can use the createReactAgent utility to skip much of the boilerplate code from
the previous example.

10.4. Adding checkpointers in createReactAgent()

By default, the agents built with the createReactAgent() utility don't have any memory thread support.

For example, if we take the previous agent it will not be able to remember the user's previous inquiries during a single conversation:

```
await agent.invoke({
  messages: [
    new HumanMessage("Add 10 and 8, then subtract 2"
      + " from the result." )
  ]
})
// The result of adding 10 and 8 is 18,
// and subtracting 2 from that result gives 16.

await agent.invoke({
  messages: [
    new HumanMessage("and add 100 to the result." ),
  ]
})
// Could you please provide the initial numbers you would
// like to add or subtract before adding 100 to the result?
```

However, this can be easily solved using the MemorySaver checkpointer for storing and recalling user queries. It's a very similar flow to the one we saw earlier, in the Threads chapter:

```
// imports, define the LLM and tools

const tools = [addTool, subtractTool]
```

```javascript
// Enable the memory saver for single-thread memory
const checkpointSaver = new MemorySaver()
const thread_id = "MATH"
const agent = createReactAgent({llm, tools, checkpointSaver})

let result = await agent.invoke({
  messages: [
    new HumanMessage("Add 10 and 8, then subtract 2 from the
result." ),
  ]
}, { configurable: { thread_id } })

console.log(getLastMessage(result).content)
// The result of adding 10 and 8 is 18.
// After subtracting 2 from 18, the final result is 16.

result = await agent.invoke({
  messages: [
    new HumanMessage("and add 100 to the result." ),
  ]
}, { configurable: { thread_id } })

console.log(getLastMessage(result).content)
// Adding 100 to the result gives us 116.
```

10.5. When ReACT Agents are not the best choice

While ReACT agents are powerful, they are not always the best solution. Here are some cases where they may not be ideal:

1. High-Speed, Low-Latency Scenarios. ReACT agents rely on an iterative reasoning loop, which can introduce delays.

2. Strictly Rule-Based Environments. Some industries require deterministic decision-making with no room for adaptive reasoning.

3. Computational Cost and Resource Constraints. Running an iterative reasoning loop can be computationally expensive.

4. When Transparency is a Liability. In security-sensitive environments, logging every decision could expose proprietary strategies.

10.6. Conclusion

In this chapter, we examined the ReACT AI architecture, its core cycle of reasoning, acting, and responding, and its implementation using LangGraph.

We also explored memory support for multi-turn interactions and discussed cases where ReACT agents might not be the best choice.

Let's now move to our next adventure in the AI Agents world!

11. Multimodal AI agents

11.1. Introduction

So far, all our examples have been based on text data. We pass in some text and receive text in return.

Many new-generation models have multimodal capabilities. By multimodality, we refer to the ability of LLMs to read and understand data in different formats, such as audio files, videos, images, and more.

This opens up many new possibilities, so let's see how we can leverage these multimodal features to expand the capabilities of AI agents!

11.2. Example Setup

The goal of this chapter is to build a ReAct AI agent capable of understanding both image and audio files.

Our agent will have access to two tools: one for processing audio files and another for processing image files. The AI agent will analyze the initial prompt and determine which tool to use.

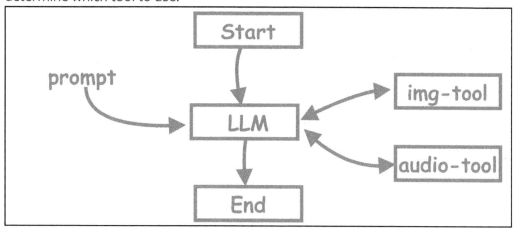

To test this functionality, I will use two different inputs:

- audio.mp3: This file contains audio extracted from a YouTube video I published about using Ollama to invoke local models.

- image.jpg: This file is a picture displaying all the ingredients needed to prepare sushi.

Below is the final file and folder structure we will have by the end of this example:

```
/multimodal-agent
│   ├── /tools
│   │   ├── audio-tool.js
│   │   ├── image-tool.js
│   ├── .env
│   ├── agent.js
│   ├── audio.mp3
│   ├── image.jpg
│   ├── package-lock.json
│   └── package.json
```

11.3. Building an Image Processing Tool

AI agents can now process and interpret images, allowing them to extract meaningful insights from visual data.

In this section, we introduce a multimodal tool that enables our LangGraph powered AI agent to analyze images using OpenAI's GPT-4o. This tool reads an image file, encodes it, and passes it to the LLM for analysis.

Below is the full code of the tool:

```js
// FILE: tools/image-tool.js
import { tool } from "@langchain/core/tools"
import { z } from "zod"
import { ChatOpenAI } from "@langchain/openai"
import fs from 'fs'
import * as dotenv from "dotenv"
import { HumanMessage } from "@langchain/core/messages"

dotenv.config({ path: '../.env' })

const readImageFileSchema = z.object({
    filePath: z.string().describe("The file name of the picture.")
})

const readImageFileTool = tool(
    async ({ filePath }) => {
        const model = new ChatOpenAI({
            modelName: "gpt-4o", maxTokens: 1000
  })

        const imageData =
fs.readFileSync(filePath).toString("base64")
```

```
        const imageDataUrl = "data:image/jpeg;base64," + imageData

        const messages = [new HumanMessage({ content: [
            {
                "type": "text",
                "text": "What does this image contain?"
            },
            {
                "type": "image_url",
                "image_url": {
                    "url": imageDataUrl
                }
            }
        ]})]

        const response = await model.invoke(messages)
        return response.content
    },
    {

    name: "readImageFileTool",
    description: "Reads the content of an image file.",
    schema: readImageFileSchema,

    }
)

export default readImageFileTool
```

The readImageFileTool does the following:

1. takes a file path as input

2. loads the image and converts it to base64-encoded data

3. passes the encoded data to an LLM for analysis

One thing to note is that the readImageFileSchema acts as a guardrail, ensuring that only valid file paths are passed to the tool.

Using this tool, our LangGraph based AI agent can now analyze images, whether extracting context from screenshots, identifying objects, or summarizing diagrams as easy as processing text.

Let's now explore how we can do the same thing with audio files.

11.4. Using Open AI Whisper to process audio files

As in the case of images, AI agents can now listen, transcribe, and analyze audio files, enabling new ways to process spoken information.

OpenAI Whisper, launched in September 2022, is a powerful automatic speech recognition (ASR) system designed to transcribe and understand spoken human language.

The JavaScript code below defines an audio processing tool that enables a LangGraph-powered AI agent to transcribe and analyze audio content using OpenAI Whisper and GPT-4o.

```
// FILE: tools/audio-tool.js
import { tool } from "@langchain/core/tools"
import { z } from "zod"
import { ChatOpenAI } from "@langchain/openai"
import {
  OpenAIWhisperAudio
} from
"@langchain/community/document_loaders/fs/openai_whisper_audio"
import * as dotenv from "dotenv"
dotenv.config({ path: '../.env' })


const readAudioFileSchema = z.object({
    filePath: z.string().describe("The file name of the audio
file.")
})


const readAudioFileTool = tool(
    async ({ filePath }) => {
      const model = new ChatOpenAI({
        model: "gpt-4o",
```

```
      temperature: 0
    })

    const loader = new OpenAIWhisperAudio(filePath, {
      transcriptionCreateParams: {
        language: "en",
      }
    })

    const docs = await loader.load()

    const transcript = docs[0].pageContent

    const response = await model.invoke("Describe what the"+
      + " following audio transcript is about: \n"
      + transcript)
    return response.content
  },
  {
      name: "readAudioFileTool",
      description: "Reads the content of an audio file.",
      schema: readAudioFileSchema,
  }
)

export default readAudioFileTool
```

One cool thing about Whisper is that it already knows, out of the box, how to handle different languages, accents, background noise, and more.

Our use case in this example will be simpler, but with this tool, LangGraph agents can now process spoken content, enabling applications such as:

- meeting note generation

- podcast summarization

- voice memo transcription

In the next section, we'll explore how to use an AI agent to integrate these two multi-modal tools and process various types of files.

11.5. Bringing It All Together - A Multimodal AI Agent with LangGraph

In this final section, we bring together our image analysis tool and audio transcription tool to create a multimodal LangGraph AI agent. This agent can process images and audio files, extract insights, and respond with concise summaries.

This multimodal AI agent combines text, audio, and images into a single processing pipeline.

Below is the full code:

```
import { HumanMessage, SystemMessage } from
"@langchain/core/messages"
import { ToolNode } from "@langchain/langgraph/prebuilt"
import {
  END, MessagesAnnotation, START, StateGraph
} from "@langchain/langgraph"
import { ChatOpenAI } from "@langchain/openai"
import * as dotenv from "dotenv"
import { readAudioFileTool, readImageFileTool } from
"./tools/index.js"
dotenv.config({ path: '../.env' })

const llm = new ChatOpenAI({ model: "gpt-4o", temperature: 0 })

const getLastMessage = ({ messages }) => messages[messages.length
- 1]

const tools = [readImageFileTool, readAudioFileTool]
const toolNode = new ToolNode(tools)
const llmWithTools = llm.bindTools(tools)
```

```javascript
const callModel = async (state) => {
  const { messages } = state
  const result = await llmWithTools.invoke(messages)
  return { messages: [result] }
}


const shouldContinue = (state) => {
  const lastMessage = getLastMessage(state)
  const didAICalledAnyTools = lastMessage._getType() === "ai" &&
    lastMessage.tool_calls?.length
  return didAICalledAnyTools ? "tools" : END
}

const graph = new StateGraph(MessagesAnnotation)
 .addNode("agent", callModel)
 .addNode("tools", toolNode)
 .addEdge(START, "agent")
 .addEdge("tools", "agent")
 .addConditionalEdges("agent", shouldContinue, ["tools", END])

const runnable = graph.compile()
```

The AI agent uses a plain ReACT architecture, as we have used before in other examples. Based on the information it receives from the input prompt, it will decide to call one tool or another.

It's now time to see our agent in action. Let's first test it out using an image file.

```
const result = await runnable.invoke({
  messages: [
    new SystemMessage("You are responsible for answering user"
      + " questions using tools. Respond as short as possible"),
    new HumanMessage("What's in the file named image.jpg ?" )
  ]
})

console.log(getLastMessage(result).content)
```

I will invoke it using an image that contains all the ingredients needed to make a sushi dish:

The file "image.jpg" contains an image of sushi ingredients, including rice, seaweed, avocado, wasabi, soy sauce, vinegar, pickled ginger, sugar, salt, and salmon.

Now that this works, is now time to test it out also with an audio file.

I have an audio mp3 file containing the audio from a YouTube tutorial I posted on how to use Ollama to run local LLMs:

```
const result = await runnable.invoke({
  messages: [
    new SystemMessage("You are responsible for answering user"
      + " questions using tools. Respond as short as possible"),
    new HumanMessage("What's in the file named audio.mp3 ?" ),
  ]
})

console.log(getLastMessage(result).content)
```

If we run the above code we will get this output:

By the way, if you are interested to check out this tutorial, you can see it here youtu.be/pKK07kObVnw.

11.6. Conclusion

And that's it! We have just built a multimodal AI agent capable of understanding text, images, and audio. This isn't just an abstract concept—it's a practical, working AI that can see, listen, and respond just like a human assistant would.

The future of AI is multimodal, and with LangGraph, we're already there!

12. About the Author

Hi there, friend! I'm Daniel, a software developer and educator.

I like computers. I try to make them like me back. More than computers I like humans. I think every person has value, intelligence, and good inside. I believe that education is the key to building a better, stable, and richer world.

I used to work at companies such as Skillshare, Tradeshift and ING, where I had a chance to be exposed to completely different types of frontend development in various teams.

Over the past five years, I've been writing articles on js-craft.io about JavaScript, CSS, and other software development topics.

I've always enjoyed teaching, holding both in-class and online classes, and being involved in tech education startups.

You can always reach me at daniel@js-craft.io, and read more about me at https://www.js-craft.io/about/.

You can find me also on:

- GitHub: github.com/daniel-jscraft
- Twitter: @js_craft_hq
- Mastdotodn: @daniel_js_craft
- YouTube: @js-craftacademy6740

13. Final Words

I hope you've enjoyed reading this book!

I'd love to hear your thoughts—what worked for you and what didn't so I can make future versions even better.

Feel free to reach out anytime at daniel@js-craft.io for updated versions, the code samples or if you think there are more topics I should cover.

And if you liked the book, leaving a review would mean a lot to me.

Thanks for sticking around, and as always, keep coding!

www.ingramcontent.com/pod-product-compliance
Lightning Source LLC
LaVergne TN
LVHW081528050326
832903LV00025B/1685